SCHOLASTIC
ENGLISH SKILLS

Comprehension
Workbook

Ages 7–8

SCHOLASTIC
ENGLISH SKILLS

Comprehension

Scholastic Education, an imprint of Scholastic Ltd
Book End, Range Road, Witney, Oxfordshire, OX29 0YD
Registered office: Westfield Road, Southam,
Warwickshire CV47 0RA
www.scholastic.co.uk

© 2016, Scholastic Ltd

23456789 6789012345

British Library Cataloguing-in-Publication Data
A catalogue record for this book is available from the British Library.

ISBN 978-1407-14179-4

Printed and bound in Great Britain by Ashford Colour Press Ltd.

Acknowledgements

The publishers gratefully acknowledge permission to reproduce the following copyright material: **Andersen Press Ltd** for the use of text and an illustration from *Robot Rumpus* by Sean Taylor and Ross Collins. Text © 2013, Sean Taylor. Illustration © 2013, Ross Collins. (2013, Andersen Press Ltd); text and an illustration from *Dr Xargle's Book of Earth Tiggers* by Jeanne Willis and Tony Ross. Text © 1990, Jeanne Willis. Illustration © 1990, Tony Ross. (1990, Andersen Press Ltd); text and illustrations from *Drat That Cat!* by Tony Ross. Text and illustrations © 2013, Tony Ross. (2013, Andersen Press Ltd); text and illustration from *Frog and the Stranger* by Max Velthuijs. Text and illustration © 1993, Max Velthuijs Foundation. (1993, Andersen Press Ltd); text and illustration from *Frog is a Hero* by Max Velthuijs. Text and illustration © 1995, Max Velthuijs Foundation. (1995, Andersen Press Ltd). **Bloomsbury Publishing Plc** for the use of the cover of *Mole and the Baby Bird* by Marjorie Newman and Patrick Benson. Text © 2002, Marjorie Newman. Illustration © 2002, Patrick Benson. (2002, Bloomsbury Publishing Plc); text and illustration from *There's a Lion in my Cornflakes* by Michelle Robinson and Jim Field. Text © 2014, Michelle Robinson. Illustration © 2014, Jim Field. (2014, Bloomsbury Publishing Plc). **David Higham Associates** for the use of text from *Mairi's Mermaid* by Michael Morpurgo. Text © 2001, Michael Morpurgo. (2001, Egmont UK Ltd). **Frances Lincoln Children's Books** for permission to use text and illustrations from *Bob and Rob* by Sue Pickford. Text and illustrations © 2013, Sue Pickford. (2013,

Frances Lincoln Children's Books). **Kids Can Press Ltd** for the use of text and illustrations from *Scaredy Squirrel at the Beach* by Mélanie Watt. Text and illustrations © 2008, Mélanie Watt. (2009, Kids Can Press Ltd, Toronto). **Colin McNaughton** for the use of text and illustrations from *Football Crazy* by Colin McNaughton. Text and illustrations © Colin McNaughton, 1980. (1980, William Heinemann Ltd). **Raintree Publishers** for the use of an illustration from *Flood* by Alvaro F. Villa. © 2013, Capstone Young Readers. (2014, Curious Fox, an imprint of Capstone Global Library Limited). **Macmillan Children's Books** for permission to use text and illustrations from *The Gruffalo* by Julia Donaldson, illustrated by Axel Scheffler. Text © 1999, Julia Donaldson. Illustrations © 1999 Axel Scheffler. (1999, Macmillan Children's Books); text and illustrations from *The Gruffalo's Child* by Julia Donaldson, illustrated by Axel Scheffler. Text © 2004, Julia Donaldson. Illustrations © 2004, Axel Scheffler. (2004, Macmillan Children's Books). **Random House Children's Books** for permission to use text and illustrations from *Serpents and Scarecrows* by Alfie Small. Text and illustrations © 2013, Alfie Small. (2013, David Fickling Books); text and illustrations from *Traction Man and the Beach Odyssey* by Mini Grey. Text and illustrations © 2011, Mini Grey. (2011, Jonathan Cape). **Scholastic Children's Books** for the use of text and an illustration from *The Lighthouse Keeper's Lunch* by Ronda and David Armitage. Text © 1994, Ronda Armitage. Illustration © 1994, David Armitage. (1977, Andre Deutsch Ltd); text and illustrations from *Dinosaurs* by Philip Ardagh, illustrated by Mike Gordon. Text © 2009, Philip Ardagh. Illustration © 2009, Mike Gordon. (2009, Scholastic Ltd); text and an illustration from *Horrible Geography of the World* by Anita Ganeri. Text © 2007, Anita Ganeri. Illustration © 2007, Mike Phillips. (2007, Scholastic Ltd); text and an illustration from *The Lighthouse Keeper's Catastrophe* by Ronda and David Armitage. Text © 1998, Ronda Armitage. Illustration © 1998, David Armitage. (1998, Scholastic Ltd). **Walker Books Ltd** for the use of the cover, a text extract and illustrations from *A First Book of Nature* by Nicola Davies, illustrated by Mark Hearld. Text © 2012, Nicola Davies. Illustrations © 2012, Mark Hearld. (2012, Walker Books Ltd); text and an illustration from *Charley's First Night* by Amy Hest, illustrated by Helen Oxenbury. Text © 2012, Amy Hest. Illustrations © 2012, Helen Oxenbury. (2012, Walker Books Ltd); text and illustrations from *Just Ducks* by Nicola Davies, illustrated by Salvatore Rubbino. Text © 2012, Nicola Davies. Illustrations © 2012, Salvatore Rubbino. (2012, Walker Books Ltd); text and illustrations from *Knuffle Bunny* by Mo Willems. Text and illustrations © 2005, Mo Willems. (2005, Walker Books Ltd); text and illustrations from *The Woman Who Won Things* by Allan Ahlberg, illustrated by Katharine McEwen. Text © 2002, Allan Ahlberg. Illustrations © 2002, Katharine McEwen. (2002, Walker Books Ltd).

Every effort has been made to trace copyright holders for the works reproduced in this book, and the publishers apologise for any inadvertent omissions.

Author Donna Thomson
Editorial Rachel Morgan, Anna Hall, Kate Soar, Margaret Eaton
Consultants Hilarie Medler, Libby Allman

Cover and Series Design Neil Salt and Nicolle Thomas
Layout K & S Design
Illustration Gemma Hastilow-Smith
Cover Illustration Eddie Rego

Contents

How to use this book

- *Scholastic English Skills Workbooks* help your child to practise and improve their skills in English.

- The content is divided into chapters that relate to different skills. The final 'Review' chapter contains a mix of questions that bring together all of these skills. These questions increase in difficulty as the chapter progresses.

- Keep the working time short and come back to an activity if your child finds it too difficult. Ask your child to note any areas of difficulty. Don't worry if your child does not 'get' a concept first time, as children learn at different rates and content is likely to be covered at different times throughout the school year.

- Find out more information about comprehension skills and check your child's answers at www.scholastic.co.uk/ses/comprehension.

- Give lots of encouragement, complete the 'How did you do' for each activity and the progress chart as your child finishes each chapter.

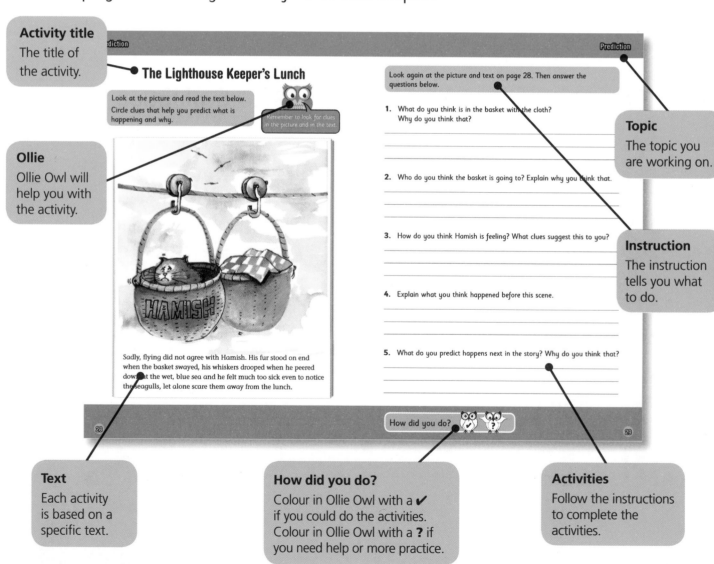

Activity title
The title of the activity.

Ollie
Ollie Owl will help you with the activity.

Text
Each activity is based on a specific text.

How did you do?
Colour in Ollie Owl with a ✔ if you could do the activities. Colour in Ollie Owl with a ? if you need help or more practice.

Activities
Follow the instructions to complete the activities.

Topic
The topic you are working on.

Instruction
The instruction tells you what to do.

If you need help, ask an adult!

Retelling – character, action and place

Read the beginning of *The Gruffalo*, which is shown below. Underline the 'who', 'what' and 'where' words in the text using different coloured pens.

Who is in the story?
What are they doing?
Where are they?

A mouse took a stroll through the deep dark wood.
A fox saw the mouse and the mouse looked good.
"Where are you going to, little brown mouse?
Come and have lunch in my underground house."
It's terribly kind of you, Fox, but no —
I'm going to have lunch with a gruffalo."

"He has terrible tusks, and terrible claws,

And terrible teeth in his terrible jaws."

"A gruffalo? What's a gruffalo?"
"A gruffalo! Why, didn't you know?"

"Where are you meeting him?"
"Here, by these rocks,
And his favourite food is roasted fox."

Use the information you have underlined to help you to retell the beginning of this story in your own words. The first line has been given to you to help you get started...

This story is about...

Re-read the beginning of *The Gruffalo* on page 5. Use the information you have underlined on the last page to answer the questions below.

1. What is the main theme of the story?

   _____

   _____

   _____

2. Who takes a stroll and meets a fox?

   _____

3. Where do the main characters meet?

   _____

4. What does the mouse say when the fox invites him to lunch?

   _____

5. Where does the fox live?

   _____

6. What does the mouse say about the gruffalo that might scare off the fox?

   _____

   _____

   _____

How did you do?

What's the problem?

Read the extract below from the story *Mairi's Mermaid*. Underline or circle the clues that suggest the possible problems and solution in the story.

Look for **who** and **what** the story is about.

Mairi still could not swim. She wished she could, but she just couldn't.

I'm sinking again!

All the holidays she'd been trying, but every time she took her feet off the bottom she sank like a stone.

Her brother Robbie swam like a fish. 'It's easy,' he told her. 'You believe in mermaids don't you? Well, just pretend you're a mermaid, like this.'

He doesn't even have armbands.

How do you think Mairi solves the problem in the end?
Draw or write the solution to Mairi's problem in the box below.

Re-read the story on page 7 and answer the questions below.

1. Who is having a problem in the story?

_____

2. The main character has more than one problem, so can you name two problems?

_____

_____

3. What does Robbie think will solve the problem?

_____

4. What does the title of the story suggest might happen in the end?

_____

_____

Now write two of your own questions and answers about the text.

Your question: _____

_____

Your answer: _____

_____

Your question: _____

_____

Your answer: _____

_____

How did you do?

How to plant spring bulbs

Read the instructions below that tell you how to plant spring bulbs.

1. Lay gravel in the base of a 12cm pot.

2. Half fill the pot with compost.

3. Lay the bulbs on the surface of the soil.

4. Cover the bulbs with compost and water.

5. Leave the pot in a dark place until the shoots appear. You will need to keep checking the pot.

6. Bring the bulbs into the light, keep them watered and watch them grow.

In the table below, rewrite the instructions from page 9 using your own words. Make sure they are in the correct order.

1. First...	2. Next...
3. Now...	4. Then...
5. After that...	6. Finally...

Answer the question below. Then write your own question and answer using the planting instructions.

Question: What do you need to do first when planting spring bulbs?
Answer: _____

Your question: _____
_____
Your answer: _____
_____

How did you do?

Scaredy Squirrel at the beach

Scaredy Squirrel wants to visit the beach for the first time to collect shells. Read about his plan below.

MISSION: Operation Seashell

7:00 a.m.:   Enter box and wait (don't forget passport)

7:30 a.m.:   Get picked up by mail van (verify passport)

8:42 a.m.:   Arrive at beach and wait until the coast is clear (don't lose passport)

11:42 a.m.:   Exit box and find seashell (hold passport)

1:49 p.m.:   Enter box and wait for pick-up (check passport)

6:00 p.m.:   Get delivered back to nut tree (put away passport)

Now read the story below about what actually happened.

Do you think Scaredy Squirrel's day went to plan? What do you think happens in the end?

The next morning, as planned, Scaredy Squirrel jumps into the box.

At 7:30 a.m. he gets picked up. They drive... and drive.

At 8:42 a.m. Scaredy gets dropped off and waits... and waits.

But at 11:42 a.m. a crowd appears!

People were NOT part of the plan!

Scaredy Squirrel panics and plays dead.

Two hours later, he opens his eyes to find a perfect seashell right under his nose, and he is surrounded by friendly people. He decides to join the crowd...

Draw the beginning, middle and end of the story on page 11 in the correct order below. Next to each picture, explain what happened.

Think about the order of events in the story.

Beginning: The story is about... (Who? What? Where?)

_____

_____

_____

_____

Middle: The problem is...

_____

_____

_____

_____

End: I think what happens in the end is...

_____

_____

_____

_____

Now retell what happens in the story out loud from the beginning to the end.

How did you do?

Asking 'who' questions

Use the information about the characters below to complete the 'who' questions and answers. Then write your own question and answer.

'**Who**' questions ask about the characters in a story.

Meet The Gaskitts
(and Horace's friend)

Mrs Gaskitt
A taxi-driver
and loving mother
who likes to enter
competitions.

Mr Gaskitt
A fond hard-working
father who always
takes any job
he can get.

Gus and Gloria Gaskitt
Nine-and-a-half-year-old twins.

Question: Who is nine and a half years old?
Answer: _____

Your 'who' question: _____
Answer: Mrs Gaskitt is a taxi-driver.

Your 'who' question: _____
Your answer: _____

Use the information below to answer the 'who' question.
Then write your own 'who' questions and answers.

Mrs Gaskitt's Luck Runs Out

It was a warm May evening.
Mrs Gaskitt walked home
with her children,
her cat and her prizes.
Gus and Gloria were telling
their mum all about Mrs Plum.

POST

Good evening, Mrs Gaskitt!

*Mum, Plum –
that rhymes!*

1st PRIZE

Question: Who walked home with her children, her prizes and the cat?
Answer: _____

Your 'who' question: _____
_____
Your answer: _____

Your 'who' question: _____
_____
Your answer: _____

How did you do?

Asking 'what' questions

Look at the pictures and read the text below.
Circle what Bruno is doing on each day.
Monday has been done for you.

'**What**' questions ask about the characters' actions in a story.

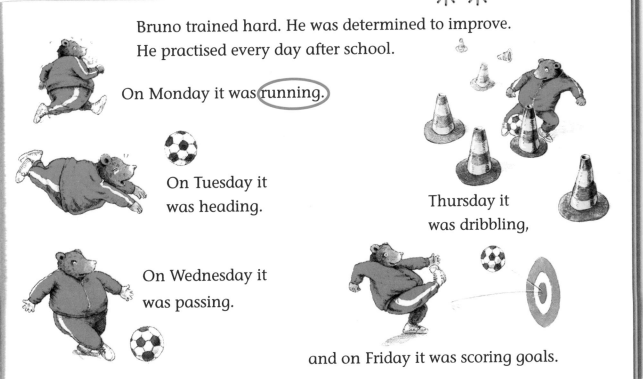

Bruno trained hard. He was determined to improve.
He practised every day after school.

On Monday it was running.

On Tuesday it was heading.

On Wednesday it was passing.

Thursday it was dribbling,

and on Friday it was scoring goals.

Read the example below and then answer the question.

Example:
Question: What does Bruno do after school?
Answer: Bruno does football training after school.

Question: What does Bruno do to improve his football skills?
Answer: _____

Use the text on page 15 to help you answer the questions below.

1. What training does Bruno do on Monday?

_____

2. What does Bruno do on the second day of the week?

_____

3. What does Bruno do to improve his football skills on a Thursday?

_____

Now write three of your own 'what' questions and answers about the text on page 15.

Your 'what' question: _____

_____

Your answer: _____

Your 'what' question: _____

_____

Your answer: _____

Your 'what' question: _____

_____

Your answer: _____

How did you do?

Asking 'where' questions

Look at the scene and read the text below from *Traction Man and the Beach Odyssey*. Circle where the characters are in the picture.

'**Where**' questions ask about the location of characters and items in a story.

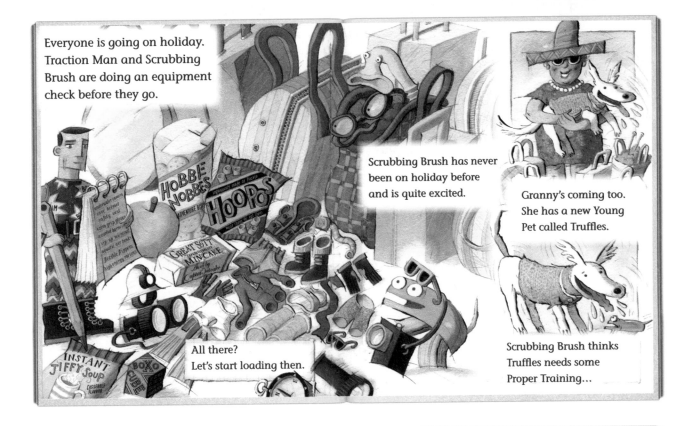

Everyone is going on holiday. Traction Man and Scrubbing Brush are doing an equipment check before they go.

Scrubbing Brush has never been on holiday before and is quite excited.

Granny's coming too. She has a new Young Pet called Truffles.

All there? Let's start loading then.

Scrubbing Brush thinks Truffles needs some Proper Training...

Look carefully at the picture. See if you can find all the items in the box below.

binoculars   flippers   jacket

gloves   helmet with headlight   camera

air tanks   compass   potato snacks

mask   sunglasses   snorkel   shorts

Can you see any other items in the scene?

Use information about the characters and objects in the story on page 17 to ask and answer 'where' questions. How many of the words in the box below can you use? One has been done for you.

on   inside   under   below   opposite   by

~~in front of~~   next to   near   beside   behind

Example:

Question: Where is Traction Man?

Answer: Traction Man is standing **in front of** his equipment.

Question: _____

Answer: The sunglasses are sitting on Scrubbing Brush's head.

Question: Where are the binoculars?

Answer: _____
_____

Question: Where is Traction Man's snorkel?

Answer: _____
_____

Question: Where is Traction Man's helmet?

Answer: _____
_____

Now write four of your own 'where' questions and answers about the people or things in the picture on page 17. Use the words in the box on page 18 to help you.

Your 'where' question: _____

_____

Your answer: _____

_____

Your 'where' question: _____

_____

Your answer: _____

_____

Your 'where' question: _____

_____

Your answer: _____

_____

Your 'where' question: _____

_____

Your answer: _____

_____

How did you do?

Key words – character, action and place

Read the text below. Underline **who** the information is about, **what** they are doing and **where** they are. Then place the words you've underlined in the correct column in the table. One row has been done for you.

In Spring, there won't be so many ducks on the way home, 'cos they'll be busy nesting. For almost a month, the mother ducks will sit on their eggs, hidden away, sometimes in some pretty funny places.

Mallard ducks make their nests on the ground and lay between 8 and 13 eggs.

Predators like to eat eggs and ducklings so mother ducks hide their nests carefully.

Last year, one made her nest in our greenhouse! When the ducklings hatched...

Who	What (doing)	Where
Mother ducks	sit on their eggs	in some pretty funny places.

Re-read the text on page 20 and answer the questions below.

1. Who will be busy nesting in spring?

_____

2. What do mother ducks do for almost a month?

_____

3. Where do mother ducks hide when they are nesting?

_____

4. Where do mallard ducks make their nests?

_____

Now write three of your own 'who', 'what' and 'where' questions and answers using the information you have underlined on page 20.

Your 'who' question: _____

Your answer: _____

Your 'what' question: _____

Your answer: _____

Your 'where' question: _____

Your answer: _____

How did you do?

Serpents and Scarecrows

Look at the pictures and read the text below from *Serpents and Scarecrows*.

Think about what is happening in the story.
What do you think will happen next?
Why do you think this?

Snakes Alive!

"SSSSS!" hissed the fork-tongued serpent. "I'll ssqueeze you until you ssqueak, you insssufferable ssquirts!"

"Let go," I gasped, feeling his thick, scaly body tighten around me. "I'm not a tube of toothpaste."

"Won't!" snapped the bad-tempered snake, tightening his grip even more.

Things in my explorer's rucksack

Dinosaur tooth
string
Water bottle
GLUE
Glue pen
Scissors
Magnifying glass
Book of interesting facts
EXPLORER'S HANDBOOK
MR. ITCHY!
Itching Powder
CHOCOLATE
Chocolate (very important!)
Pencils
Maps
Compass

Use the clues in the text and pictures on page 22 to help you complete the sentences below.

The item in Alfie's rucksack that might save him from the snake is

_____

I think this because _____

_____

Draw a picture of what you think happens next in the story and explain why you think this.

I think this happens next because _____

_____

_____

_____

_____

How did you do?

Jack be nimble

Read the nursery rhyme below aloud. Underline the words that rhyme.

Jack be nimble,

Jack be quick,

Jack jumped over a candlestick.

Jack jumped high,

Jack jumped low,

Jack jumped over and burned his toe.

Now read aloud another version of the nursery rhyme.
Fill in the missing words using rhyming words from the box below. You won't need to use all of the words.

higher   bin   sick   candlestick   bicycle   toe   foot

Jack was nimble,

Jack was quick,

Jack jumped over a _____.

Jack was silly,

Jack jumped _____,

Jack jumped over a roaring fire.

Jack was nimble,

Jack was thin,

Jack jumped over our rubbish _____.

Jack was lazy,

And sometimes slow,

Jack tripped over and stubbed his _____.

Complete the following verses using rhyming words.

Jack is nimble,
Jack is fast,
But when he races he still comes _____.

Jack is nimble,
Jack is small,
Jack rolls down the hill,
In a tight little _____.

Jack is nimble,
Jack is wild,
Jack jumps over another _____.

Jack is nimble,
Jack is brave,
Jack jumps over a bear in his _____.

Jack is silly,
Jack is mad,
Jack jumps over his poor old _____.

He does this once,
He does this again,
Then jumps over a line of _____.

Jack is cool,
He doesn't fuss,
Jack jumps over a big red _____.

How did you do?

Book covers

Look at the two book covers. Tick the box next to the one you think is a fiction book. Then complete the sentence to explain why you think this.

Think about what the books are about. What clues are there that tell you this?

I think the book I have chosen is fiction because...

_____
_____
_____
_____
_____
_____
_____
_____

How did you do?

Creating covers

Choose one of the titles below and draw your own book cover. Then answer the questions below.

Think about whether your book is fiction or non-fiction. What effect will this have on your cover?

The Amazing House on the Hill	Crazy about Climbing
Pets Messy Martin	Elephant Family Too Small

1. What sort of book do you think this is? Why do you say that?

_____

_____

2. What do you think the story is about?

_____

_____

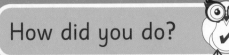 How did you do?

The Lighthouse Keeper's Lunch

Look at the picture and read the text below.
Circle clues that help you predict what is happening and why.

Remember to look for clues in the picture and in the text.

Sadly, flying did not agree with Hamish. His fur stood on end when the basket swayed, his whiskers drooped when he peered down at the wet, blue sea and he felt much too sick even to notice the seagulls, let alone scare them away from the lunch.

Look again at the picture and text on page 28. Then answer the questions below.

1. What do you think is in the basket with the cloth?
    Why do you think that?

    _____

    _____

    _____

2. Who do you think the basket is going to? Explain why you think that.

    _____

    _____

    _____

3. How do you think Hamish is feeling? What clues suggest this to you?

    _____

    _____

    _____

4. Explain what you think happened before this scene.

    _____

    _____

    _____

5. What do you predict happens next in the story? Why do you think that?

    _____

    _____

    _____

How did you do?

Robot Rumpus

Look at the picture and read the text. Underline the 'who', 'what' and 'where' words in different colours.

Then write out some questions that PC Page would ask using the information you have underlined. One has been done for you.

PC Page is always looking out for literal clues. She notes down the '**who**', '**what**' and '**where**' information that is right there on the page.

My mum and dad are busy.
So just last night they said,
"We decided to buy these fantastic robots to get you into bed."

Example:

PC Page question:

Who is busy?

PC Page question:

_____

_____

PC Page question:

_____

_____

PC Page question:

_____

_____

Now circle the **inference** clues on the page that help you think more deeply about the girl, her family and what is happening.

Use the picture and text on page 30 to answer the questions below.

Tick the PC Page box if it is a **literal** question.

Tick the Text Detective box if it is an **inference** question.

Literal answers are right there in the picture and text. **Inference** answers link to clues in the story.

Question	PC Page	Text Detective
Who bought the robots? _____	☐	☐
Why did they buy her the robots? _____ _____	☐	☐
Where was the girl when she was told about the robots? _____	☐	☐
Do you think the girl is an only child? Why do you think that? _____ _____	☐	☐
Do the girl's parents think the robots are amazing? Why do you think that? _____ _____	☐	☐
Do the family have a pet? Why do you think that? _____	☐	☐

How did you do?

What am I?

Read the poem below. Circle the clues in the words and picture that suggest what the poem is about and what is happening.

Think about how you know what is happening in the poem.

Swirling white in the darkness,
Dusting rooftops on the way,
Throws a blanket on the landscape,
Wrapping sounds up as it lays.

Glistening morning, hushed and bright,
Reveals the secrets at first light...
Frozen clues left in the white
Of busy creatures in the night.

Re-read the poem on page 32 and then answer the questions below. Underline the clues in the questions to help you.

1. What is happening in the first line of the poem? How do you know that?

_____

I know this because _____

2. Does the snow settle everywhere? Explain how you know.

_____

because _____

3. Is it quiet after heavy snowfall? How do you know that?

_____

_____

_____

4. What clues are left in the snow in the morning? Explain how you know.

_____

_____

Now write your own detective question and answer about the poem.

Your detective question: _____

_____

Your answer: _____

_____

How did you do?

33

Because... Bob and Rob

Circle the clues in the picture below that explain what Rob likes doing and why.

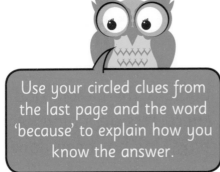

Re-read the text on page 34 and answer the questions below.

Then write your own detective question and answer.

Use your circled clues from the last page and the word 'because' to explain how you know the answer.

1. Is Rob a burglar? How do you know that?

_____

_____

_____

2. Why does Rob leave banana skins on pavements?

_____

_____

3. Why does Bob ring people's doorbells?

_____

_____

4. Why does Rob set off fire alarms in cafes?

_____

_____

Your detective question: _____

_____

Your answer: _____

_____

How did you do?

There's a Lion in My Cornflakes

Look at the picture and text below. Circle the clues that suggest what the characters are doing, where they are and why. Then write the clues in the box. One has been done for you.

Me and my brother, Dan, made umpteen trips to the supermarket and spent a whole year's pocket money on cereal.

Clues

cereal

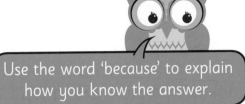

Look again at the picture and text on page 36. Use the clues you found to help you answer the questions below.

Use the word 'because' to explain how you know the answer.

1. Who bought boxes and boxes of cereal? How do you know that?

_____

_____

2. Why did the boys buy trolley loads of cornflake packets?

_____

_____

3. What did Dan and his brother have to do to get a free lion? Explain how you know that.

_____

_____

Now write two of your own detective questions and answers below.

Your detective question: _____

_____

Your answer: _____

_____

Your detective question: _____

_____

Your answer: _____

_____

How did you do?

Flood

Look at the picture and read the text below.

Underline the words in the text that have more than one meaning.
Two have been done for you.

A bolt of lightning across the sky warns us the storm is close. It is <u>spring</u>. Every year at this time we battle for days with wind and heavy rain from light till dusk. Sometimes the <u>flat</u> wet land surrounding us cannot soak up all the rain and it floods. So we make a bank of stones around our house to block the rising water.

Write each of the words you have underlined next to its two possible meanings in the table. The first two have been done for you.

Meanings	Word from text
season/coil	spring
level/living space	flat
flash/screw	
ground/arrive	

Meanings	Word from text
bright/lamp	
stop/wooden brick	
wall/place for saving money	

Use the text on page 38 to help you answer the questions below.

1. Tick the boxes next to any of the words below that have two meanings. The first one has been done for you and examples are given below.

    ☑ can   ☐ hope   ☐ tall

    ☐ row   ☐ saw   ☐ show

    > **Examples of two meanings for 'can':**
    >
    > When I wear armbands, I **can** swim.
    >
    > I opened the **can** and poured the lemonade into a glass.

2. Select one of the words ticked from the list above and then write two simple sentences that explain both meanings of that word.

    _____

    _____

3. What do you think the author means by 'a bolt of lightning'?

    _____

    _____

4. 'we battle for days with wind and heavy rain from light till dusk.' What does the author mean by 'light till dusk'?

    _____

    _____

    _____

How did you do?

Dr Xargle's Book of Earth Tiggers

Look at the picture and read the text. Circle the words in the text that have a similar meaning to the words in each of the boxes below.
Then write the word from the text on the line. One has been done for you.

Example:

despise	loathe
detest	dislike intensely

The word in the text is

hate.

bend	crease
tuck	gather

The word in the text is

_____

blow	breath
waft	blast

The word in the text is

_____

Earth Tiggers hate the Earth Hound. They fold in half and puff air into their waggler. Then they go into orbit with a hiss and a crackle.

Write the opposite meanings of the words below.

half _____

no _____

above _____

soft _____

Synonyms are words with similar meanings.
Antonyms are words with opposite meanings.

Look again at the text and picture on page 40 and answer the questions below. Remember to look for synonyms and antonyms in the questions and text. There's an example of this in the box below.

Example:

Question: Do Earth Tiggers <u>like</u> being with the Earth Hound? How do you know that?

Answer: No, Earth Tiggers do not <u>like</u> being with the Earth Hound because it says they '<u>hate</u> the Earth Hound'.

1. Are Earth Tiggers similar to cats? Why do you think that?

_____

_____

_____

2. When the author talks about the Earth Tigger's 'waggler', do you think she means its tail? Why do you think that?

_____

_____

_____

3. Do Earth Tiggers blast off into space like a rocket? How do you know?

_____

_____

_____

How did you do?

Dinosaurs

Remember to look at the pictures **and** the words.

Skim and scan the text and pictures below for the words in the box. Circle them when you find them. Two have been done for you.

Mighty giants

We'll put this in your dad's study with his other fossils.

Why were dinosaurs all so big, Jaggers?

They weren't all huge. Most dinosaurs were the size of rhinos, but some were as small as sheep or even chickens.

The biggest dinosaurs were some plant-eaters. They needed to be big to reach high up into the trees to eat the leaves ... and to fight off the meat-eating dinosaurs—

Who wanted to eat THEM!

The word "dinosaur" means "terrible lizard" But dinosaurs weren't lizards and lots of them weren't terrible. They just ate plants for about 20 hours a day!

8

sheep

dog

fossils

dinosaur

20 hours

rhinos

reach

Jaggers

put

lizards

terrible

size

boy

meat-eating

plant-eaters

Use the words you have underlined on page 42 to help you answer the questions below.

Remember the answers are right there in the text and pictures.

1. Who says the word 'dinosaur' means 'terrible lizard'?

_____

2. What is Jaggers doing with the fossil?

_____

3. What animal were most dinosaurs a similar size to?

_____

4. Were some of the biggest dinosaurs plant-eaters or were they all meat-eaters?

_____

5. Why did plant-eating dinosaurs need to be big?

_____

_____

Now write your own **literal** question and answer.

Your question: _____

_____

Your answer: _____

_____

How did you do?

Geese

Skim and scan the poem below to find synonyms for the words in the boxes. Draw a line to match the similar words. One has been done for you.

Synonyms are words with similar meanings. Antonyms are words with opposite meanings.

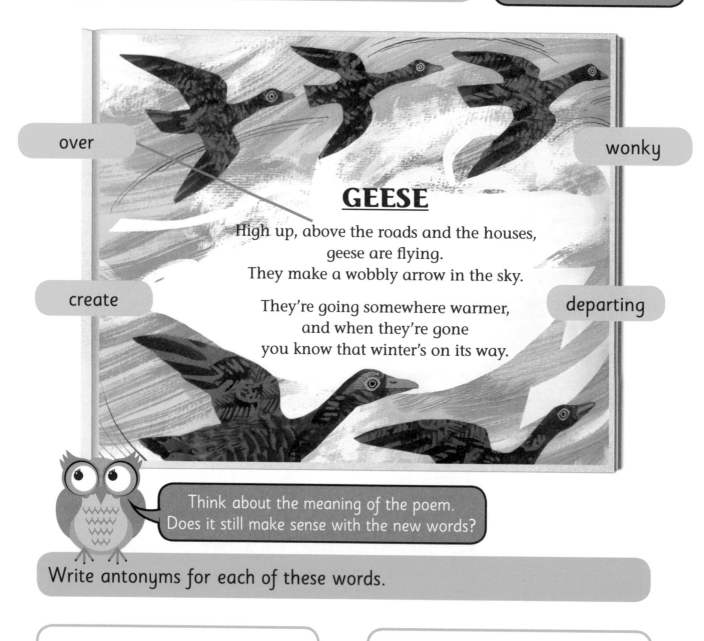

over

wonky

GEESE

High up, above the roads and the houses,
geese are flying.
They make a wobbly arrow in the sky.

They're going somewhere warmer,
and when they're gone
you know that winter's on its way.

create

departing

Think about the meaning of the poem.
Does it still make sense with the new words?

Write antonyms for each of these words.

winter _____

wonky _____

departing _____

warmer _____

Look again at the poem on page 44 and then answer the questions below. Underline the words in the questions that link to similar or opposite words in the poem.

Use the example in the box to help you.

Think carefully about the meanings of the words in the questions. Do they have any synonyms or antonyms in the poem?

Example:

Question: Are the geese flying <u>low</u> <u>over</u> <u>the land</u>? How do you know?

Answer: No, the geese are not flying low over the land because they are flying '<u>high</u> up, <u>above</u> the <u>roads</u> and the <u>houses</u>'.

---

1. Are the geese flying together in a straight line? How do you know?

_____

_____

2. Are the geese departing for a milder climate? Explain how you know.

_____

_____

Now write your own **inference** question and answer about the poem using synonyms (similar words) and antonyms (opposite words).

Your question: _____

_____

Your answer: _____

_____

How did you do?

Charley's First Night

Remember to look at the words used in the text and the expressions on the characters' faces.

Read the text and look closely at the picture. Circle the clues that suggest how the characters are feeling.

So I carried him all the way home.

I carried him in my old baby blanket, which was soft and midnight blue, and we were new together and I was very, very careful not to slip in the snow and I thought about his name. Charley. Charley Korn.

My name is Henry.

Henry Korn.

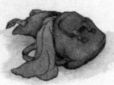

Write down what you think the characters are feeling using the information you have found in the text and pictures.

_____

_____

_____

_____

Evaluation questions have no right or wrong answer as long as you link your ideas to the information in the story.

Look again at page 46 and answer the questions below. Remember to underline the clues in the questions to help you find the answers.

1. Do you think Henry and Charley have <u>only just met</u>?
   Why do you think that?

   _____

   _____

2. What does Henry mean when he says he and Charley are 'new together'? Explain why you think that.

   _____

   _____

   _____

3. Do you think Henry really cares about Charley? Why do you think that?

   _____

   _____

   _____

   _____

4. How do you think the puppy is feeling? Give your reasons.

   _____

   _____

   _____

   _____

How did you do?

Looking for different clues

Look closely for the 'who', 'what' and 'where' information in the text and picture below. Circle clues that explain what is happening and how the characters are feeling. One has been done for you.

Then it was Saturday, the day of the match. The night before, Bruno's dreams were full of football.

"It's no fun being the substitute," he sighed at breakfast. "I do wish I was in the team."

"Who says you won't be?" said his dad. "You never know what might happen. Football's a crazy game."

"We'll be there to cheer you on, just in case you get a chance to play," said his mum.

Evaluation questions have no right or wrong answer as long as you link your ideas to the information in the story.

Look again at the picture and text on page 48 and then answer the questions below.

1. Who is having breakfast together on a Saturday morning?

_____

_____

2. Is everyone happy? How do you know that?

_____

_____

3. Why do you think Bruno is sighing?

_____

_____

4. What would Bruno like to happen? How do you know that?

_____

_____

Now write your own **evaluation** question and answer.

Your question: _____

_____

Your answer: _____

_____

How did you do?

Drat that Cat

Look at the picture and read the text. What do you think Suzy is thinking? Write the cat's thoughts in the two bubbles below.

When Mum bought a new sofa, Suzy thought
it was the best place to sharpen her claws.
Mum threw her out of the window, but she
came right back in and did it again!
"Drat that cat!"

Evaluation questions have no right or wrong answer as long as you link your ideas to the information in the story.

Use the text and picture on page 50 to help you answer the questions below.

1. How do you think Mum is feeling in the picture?
    Explain why you say that.

    _____

    _____

2. Why do you think Suzy is looking through the window?

    _____

    _____

3. Do you think Suzy minds Mum being angry with her?
    Why do you think that?

    _____

    _____

Now write your own **evaluation** question and answer from the information in the thought bubbles on page 50.

Your question: _____

_____

Your answer: _____

_____

How did you do?

Frog is a Hero

Look at the picture and read the text. Think about what is happening and why frog might be worried. In the box below, write down or draw a picture of what you think Frog might be worrying will happen.

On the fifth day, the river began to rise.

It wasn't long before water came streaming into Frog's house.

At first, Frog thought it was funny but then he began to worry.

Evaluation questions have no right or wrong answer as long as you link your ideas to the information in the story.

Answer the questions below by linking the clues in the questions with the story on page 52 and your own experience.

1. Do you think the water is likely to stop coming into Frog's house? Why do you think that?

_____

_____

2. Why do you think Frog found the situation funny at first?

_____

_____

3. Why do you think Frog's mood changed soon after the water came streaming in?

_____

_____

Now write your own **evaluation** question and answer about the information on page 52.

Your question: _____

_____

Your answer: _____

_____

How did you do?

Knuffle Bunny

Read the text and look at the pictures below.

She was even allowed to put the money into the machine.

Then they left.

Use the information on page 54 to answer the questions below.

1. What are the characters doing? Tick the correct answer.

    ☐ The characters are washing clothes.

    ☐ The characters are shopping.

2. Who put the money into the machine? Tick the correct answer.

    ☐ The little boy put the money into the machine.

    ☐ The little girl put the money into the machine.

3. How do you know that?

    _____

4. Which of the words below has a similar meaning to the word 'put'? Tick the correct answer and then write that word in the sentence below.

    ☐ place   ☐ throw   ☐ grab

    She was even allowed to _____ the money into the machine.

5. In the story, the characters leave something special behind by mistake. What do you think the object is? Why do you think it is left behind?

    _____

    _____

6. Do you think the toddler might be very upset that this object has been left behind? Why do you think that?

    _____

    _____

How did you do?

Tilly Turtle

Read the text and look at the pictures below.

Tilly Turtle

You can use...

paint

flat scourers

beads

glue

wool

buttons

paper bowl

flat sponges

Tot Tip!

Instead of beads and buttons, you can use dried beans or peas for Tilly's eyes and feet. Simply stick them in place with glue.

Bye!

19

Use the information on page 56 to answer the questions below.

1. What are we being shown how to make? Tick the correct answer.

    ☐ We are being shown how to make a tortoise.

    ☐ We are being shown how to make a turtle.

2. List the items you can use to make Tilly.

    _____

    _____

3. Can you only use beads and buttons to make Tilly's eyes?
    How do you know that?

    _____

4. Which word in the text has a similar meaning to 'paste'?

    _____

    _____

5. What do you predict the 'flat sponges' in the picture are normally used
    for? Why do you think that?

    _____

    _____

6. Do you think Tilly would be easy or difficult to make?
    Why do you think that?

    _____

    _____

    _____

How did you do?

Children's verse

Read the poem below.

JOHN AGARD

Don't Call Alligator Long-Mouth Till
You Cross River

Call alligator long-mouth
call alligator saw-mouth
call alligator pushy-mouth
call alligator scissors-mouth
call alligator raggedy-mouth
call alligator bumpy-bum
call alligator all dem rude word
but better wait
          till you cross river.

Use the information on page 58 to answer the questions below. As you are reading, try to think about the different question types.

1. What should you wait to do until after you have crossed the river?

_____

_____

2. Who is this poem about and where is it taking place?

_____

_____

3. Why might it be better to cross the river anyway?

_____

_____

4. Explain why you think the boy calls the alligator 'saw-mouth'.

_____

_____

5. Does the boy suggest these words are polite? How do you know?

_____

_____

6. What do you think might happen to the boy before he crosses the river? Why do you think that?

_____

_____

How did you do?

The Gruffalo's Child

Look at the picture and read the story below.

The Gruffalo said that no gruffalo should
Ever set foot in the deep dark wood.
"Why not? Why not?" *"Because if you do*
The Big Bad Mouse will be after you.
I met him once," said the Gruffalo.
"I met him a long long time ago."

"What does he look like? Tell us, Dad.
Is he terribly big and terribly bad?"

Use the information on page 60 to answer the questions below. As you are reading try to think about the different question types.

1. Who said they had met the Big Bad Mouse? Tick the correct answer.

   ☐ The Gruffalo

   ☐ The Gruffalo's child

2. Did they meet the Big Bad Mouse when they were young? How do you know that?

   _____

   _____

3. Which of these words has a similar meaning to the word 'Bad' in the text? Tick the correct answer and then place that word in the sentence.

   ☐ Lazy   ☐ Evil   ☐ Stupid

   'The Big _____ Mouse will be after you.'

4. Do you think the Gruffalo is making up the story about the Big Bad Mouse? Why do you say that?

   _____

   _____

   _____

5. In the story, the Gruffalo's child feels bored one day. What do you think he might decide to do next and why?

   _____

   _____

How did you do?

Frog and the Stranger

Look at the picture and read the story below.

One day, Frog decided to visit Rat. Rat was sitting resting on his new bench in the sun.
"Hello," said Frog. "I'm Frog."
"I know," said Rat. "I can see that. I'm not stupid. I can read and write and I speak three languages – English, French and German."
Frog was very impressed. Even Hare couldn't do that.

Use the information on page 62 to answer the questions below. As you are reading try to think about the different question types.

1. Who is the story about? What are they doing and where are they?

_____

_____

2. How many languages can Rat speak?

_____

3. Did Frog think Rat was cleverer than Hare? Explain how you know.

_____

_____

4. Frog saw Rat as a 'stranger'. Which of the following words has a similar meaning to the word 'stranger'? Tick the correct answer.

☐ newcomer ☐ strange ☐ explorer

5. Do you think Rat is pleased to meet Frog? Why do you think that?

_____

_____

6. What do you think might have happened before in the story? Why do you think that?

_____

_____

_____

How did you do? ✔ ?

Giganotosaurus

Look at the information on this page.

Use the information on page 64 to answer the questions below. As you are reading try to think about the different question types.

1. What sort of creature was a Giganotosaurus?

_____

2. Was the Giganotosaurus known for being the biggest hunter? Explain how you know.

_____

_____

3. What sort of clues might have been left behind to suggest the Giganotosaurus could eat very large plant-eating animals?

_____

_____

4. Do experts think the T. rex had heavier bones than the Giganotosaurus? How do you know that?

_____

_____

5. Why do you think the dinosaur was named Giganotosaurus?

_____

_____

6. Do you think T. rex might have been scared of the Giganotosaurus? Why do you think that?

_____

_____

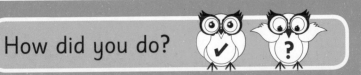

How did you do?

The Lighthouse Keeper's Catastrophe

Look at the picture and read the story below.

The spare key was exactly where Mrs Grinling said it would be – in the teapot. While she prepared cold chicken sandwiches, a fruit salad with lots of strawberries and a chocolate milkshake for his lunch, Mr Grinling listened to the midday weather forecast. It was perfectly dreadful. Wind and rain with possible thunder and lightening later in the day.
"I don't like the sound of that weather, Mrs G," said Mr Grinling. "The sooner I get back to the lighthouse, rescue Hamish and switch on the light, the happier I shall be. If you could pack the lunch in the basket I'll take it with me. Remind me to take a screwdriver, Mrs G, I have some repair work to do."

Use the information on page 66 to answer the questions below. As you are reading try to think about the different question types.

1. Who is the story about? Where are they? What are they doing?

_____

_____

_____

2. What did Mr Grinling say he needed to do at the lighthouse?

_____

3. What do you think might have happened to Hamish?
    Explain why you think that.

_____

_____

_____

4. Was there a warning on the radio that a storm was coming?
    How do you know that?

_____

_____

_____

5. Was Mr Grinling happy about the weather forecast?
    How do you know?

_____

_____

_____

6. The weather forecast was 'dreadful'. In the table below, tick one synonym and one antonym of the word 'dreadful'.

Synonym (similar word):	☐ appealing	☐ awful	☐ interesting
Antonym (opposite word):	☐ beautiful	☐ okay	☐ grim

7. Do you think that Mr and Mrs Grinling care about Hamish? Why do you think that?

_____

_____

_____

8. What do you think happens next in the story? Why do you think that?

_____

_____

_____

Now write your own question and answer about the text on page 66. Tick the box next to the type of question you have written.

☐ literal question   ☐ inference question   ☐ evaluation question

Your question: _____

_____

Your answer: _____

_____

How did you do?

Weird Wildlife

Look at the picture and read the information below.

Name: FIERCE SNAKE
Where found: Rivers and creeks.
Appearance: Yellowish body about 1.7 metres long with a black head and beady black eyes.
Reasons to avoid: The good news is the frightful fierce snake normally only poisons plague rats. Besides, it's so shy and secretive, it hardly even comes across horrible humans. The bad news is it's the most poisonous land snake and if this beauty bit you, you wouldn't stand a chance. And it's not alone. Nine out of ten of the world's deadliest snakes live in ... Australia. Very nasty.

Use the information on page 69 to answer the questions below. As you are reading try to think about the different question types.

1. What is this information about?

_____

_____

2. What is the good news about this snake?

_____

_____

_____

3. What do you think might happen if this snake bit a human? Explain why you think that.

_____

_____

_____

4. Does Australia have a large number of poisonous snakes? Give your reason for thinking that.

_____

_____

5. The fierce snake normally poisons 'plague' rats. What does the word 'plague' mean? Tick the correct meaning below.

☐ disease   ☐ poisonous   ☐ pet

Serpents and Scarecrows

Look at the pictures and read the text below from *Serpents and Scarecrows*.

Think about what is happening in the story.
What do you think will happen next?
Why do you think this?

Snakes Alive!

"SSSSS!" hissed the fork-tongued serpent. "I'll ssqueeze you until you ssqueak, you insssufferable ssquirts!"

"Let go," I gasped, feeling his thick, scaly body tighten around me. "I'm not a tube of toothpaste."

"Won't!" snapped the bad-tempered snake, tightening his grip even more.

Things in my explorer's rucksack

string

Dinosaur tooth

Water bottle

GLUE

Glue pen

Scissors

Magnifying glass

Book of interesting facts

EXPLORER'S HANDBOOK

MR. ITCHY!

CHOCOLATE

Pencils

Itching Powder

Chocolate (very important!)

Maps

Compass

Use the clues in the text and pictures on page 22 to help you complete the sentences below.

The item in Alfie's rucksack that might save him from the snake is
_____

I think this because _____
_____

Draw a picture of what you think happens next in the story and explain why you think this.

I think this happens next because _____
_____
_____
_____
_____

6. The snake is known for being 'deadly'. In the table below, tick one synonym and one antonym of the word 'deadly'.

Synonym (similar words):	☐ mean	☐ harmful	☐ upsetting
Antonym (opposite words):	☐ safe	☐ alive	☐ friendly

7. Do you feel these snakes are more frightening than other snakes? Why do you think that?

_____

_____

8. Why do you think the fierce snake might have a yellowish body?

_____

_____

Now write your own question and answer about the text on page 69. Identify the type of question you have written by ticking one of the following boxes.

☐ literal question   ☐ inference question   ☐ evaluation question

Your question: _____

_____

Your answer: _____

_____

How did you do?

71

Progress chart

Colour in Ollie when you have completed the chapter.

Retelling   1

Literal questioning   2

Prediction   3

Review   7

Evaluation   6

Clarification   5

Inference   4

CONGRATULATIONS!

Name: ....

You have completed the

Comprehension
Workbook

AGES 7–8

Age: ....   Date: ....